Windows of Deliverance on Spiritual Abuse

*How You Deal with Spirits That You Did Not
Know Were in Your Bloodline*

Janet K. Howard

NEWMAN SPRINGS PUBLISHING
320 Broad Street
Red Bank, NJ 07701

First originally published by Newman Springs Publishing 2020

ISBN 978-1-63692-022-1 (Paperback)
ISBN 978-1-63692-023-8 (Digital)

Printed in the United States of America

CONTENTS

ACKNOWLEDGMENTS

First and foremost I would like to thank God for inspiring me to write this book, because without God this book would've never been written.

I would also like to thank and forgive all the people for hurting me, because without me going through the pain of my past hurt, I would not have been able to write this book. So I forgive you.

To all the people that I've hurt in the past, those I know of and those I don't, please forgive me, because without forgiveness no one can ever move forward.

I would also like to thank my sister, Valarie. S. Taylor, for all of the days we discussed this book and all of the days you help me get to the next line with all your encouraging words. The times when I was struggling to write this book and for all the days we cried and prayed, dealing with breaking generational curses and bloodline curses. As I battled to write through the pain, wounds, and scars of my past, I was also being delivered as I wrote this book.

To my sister, Delores Murphy, for being a listening ear and taking the time out to encourage me and for keeping me uplifted before God. As I struggled through three years of being attacked, you prayed for God to strengthen me as I kept moving forward and for that I love you, sister.

To my mother, Mae Crawford, for being the loving and kind person that you are and for believing in me as I talked about writing this book, I love you for just being you. I love you forever.

To my loving auntie, Shirley Green-Douglas, for teaching me about God, and for being the other mother in my life who was always fussing when I wasn't living what you taught me and that was to live a life pleasing to God, and the thing that stuck in my head the most was that you can live for God and still have fun. And to my cousin, Tamera Green for sharing your mother with me, I love you, my cousin, forever.

To my nephew Jasper Howard for creating the most awesome cover for this book, you rock and Auntie loves you.

To my cousin James (Jay) Lopez and my son Steven Howard, for putting up with my craziness and for supporting me financially. And also to my son Sidney Jones II, for helping me when I needed you the most. Love you more than you could know.

I'd like to thank all my friends and family I didn't name because I would have to write another book just naming everyone. I love you guys.

And last but not least, to the most handsome man I know, Remoh Thompson, thank you my friend for telling me to stop procrastinating and just finish the book. Thank you also for encouraging me to love again and to keep loving. You changed my whole outlook on love. "Hey Love," the song you wrote, I hope it will encourage others. Love you always and forever my friend, Rem. T.

I hope and pray that this book will touch and change so many people's lives as this book has changed my life.

INTRODUCTION

This book is on deliverance not only for the readers, as it was born out of the author's deliverance. This book is full of vital information for your own spiritual growth. Feel free to use it for your own spiritual development. The body is a vessel; it is up to us what kind of spirit we will carry within.

Testimony of Janet K. Howard

How do you deal with spirits that you did not know we're in your bloodline? I've been spiritually abused by unseen and unknown spirits from my family bloodline, until God started revealing them to me. As I began to write this book on spiritual abuse, at first I was going to name it "Spiritual Rape," but God instructed me to change it to "Spiritual Abuse." Yes I have been spiritually raped, but it became spiritual abuse when things continued to happen to me over and over again. I didn't understand why all my life people treated me differently, and I felt rejected over and over again, mishandled, abandoned, and abused by people all my life. I began to cry out to God. I went to church looking for understanding and help so I could be healed, but I was hurt even more by the abuse the people in the church had to offer. The church is supposed to be a place of healing, the hospital for hurting souls to be healed, but instead of being healed, I was spiritually raped, emotionally raped, mentally abused, and physically wounded. So I ran from the church out into the world, looking for answers that I couldn't get in the church. But what I didn't know is that I was running into the pit, a trap that the devil had set for me. All my life Satan, the devil, was trying to kill me, and I didn't have a clue.

Even as I ran from God's calling over my life, I prayed and cried out to God, asking him why people didn't like me and why I am going through this. The Lord took me too the book of Galatians,

> Hence forth let no man trouble you, for I bare in my body the mark of the Lord Jesus Christ. Brethren, the grace of our Lord Jesus Christ, Holy Spirit be with you. (Galatians 6:17–18 NIV)

From now on don't let anyone trouble you with these things you bare on your body, the scars that show you belong to Jesus. My dear brothers and sisters, may the grace of the Lord Jesus Christ be with you all, amen. I kept running and didn't know why. I loved the Lord and I knew God's laws and commandments, but it was like something was holding me back from where my spirit really wanted to be, and it was to serve God. So I began to ask God why me? I'm not even worthy of your love, why don't you choose someone else to do your will? God answered and said, "You, I've chosen you to do my will." This made me think about when God said if we don't cry out to him, he'll get a rock to cry out for him. (God will use a rock.) How many of you know I don't want a rock crying out for me.

So you see, God will use whoever he chooses. It doesn't matter how bad our lives look to us or others, God can still use us, so I kept trying to get it right with God, but my flesh desired the things of the world. At this time I didn't know that God gives us free will to serve him, even though my spirit, heart, and soul desired to serve God my flesh was not in agreement with my soul and spirit. So I kept on sinning and doing the things the world did. I was in and out of the church. How many of you know that the devil doesn't mind about you going to church? He just doesn't want you to get saved and live for God. The devil doesn't want us to live a sin-free life, period.

So here I go again back to church. The pastor of the church had a meeting with me and told me that God wanted him to place me over the women's ministry and his wife will be helping me. So I accepted the position. It started off real good and we began to have meetings until one day a couple of the women came to me saying that they wanted me to give up my position in the women's ministry because I was too young and I wasn't married, so how was I going to teach them? So once again I allowed the devil to make me step away and stop me from doing what God called me to do. I also stopped working in the church, where the pastor had me working and showing me how to run things in the church alongside his secretary.

I kept everything inside of me—all the hurtful words and I ran, left the church running right back into the arms of the world, still not knowing it was a stronghold that needed to be broken off my life. The generational curses and bloodline curses, a spirit of Nephilim, a spirit that was holding me back. In chapters to come, I'm going to talk about spiritual husband/wife and the Nephilim spirits that the church doesn't talk about or teach us. It's a very powerful spirit that needs to be broken off the church, the people of God's lives, and how it enters in. How it needs to be broken off our lives, so it will not destroy the lives of the people who are trying to serve God. The devil comes to kill, steal, and destroy, but God comes that we might have life and that we might have it more abundantly" (John 10:10).

Kingdom living is what I do: build for God's purpose...

CHAPTER I

Spiritual Wickedness

The body is a vessel. It is up to us what kind of spirit we will carry within us.

> For we wrestle not against flesh and blood,
> but against principalities, against powers, against
> the rulers of the darkness of this world, against spir-
> itual wickedness in high places. (Ephesians 6:12)

Spiritual Rape

Spiritual Rape is when you allow your thoughts and opinions of others to affect you. It also consists of the human spirit. The natural body and the spiritual body, causing spiritual abuse, which is caused by the human spirit. These are a couple definitions of spiritual rape, but we are going to dig a little deeper into the unseen forces that the Bible speaks of in Ephesians 6:12.

Let's breakdown this scripture, "For we wrestle," there is a battle within the mind, or is it against flesh and blood, or is it against unseen powers of the darkness or some evil spirits? Let's talk about flesh and blood. The Bible clearly states that we are not wrestling with flesh and blood, but with unseen forces within our own body and the forces of darkness which is upon the Earth. Because God's children are human beings made of flesh and blood (Hebrews 2:14), the Son Jesus Christ also became flesh and blood, for only as a human being could he die and only by dying could he break the power of the devil who holds the power over death.

"Against principalities, against powers," we are describing angelic powers, good and evil, "against world of darkness, against spiritual powers of wickedness in heavenly places." "For above all principles and powers and might and dominion, and every name that is named not only in this world, but also in that which is to come" (Ephesians 1:21).

"The rulers of the darkness," is referring to the prince of this world, which is Satan or is the darkness of this present world, these evil spirits are spoken of throughout the Bible. Satan, the devil, controls the air but his powers are limited. The devil wants to enslave those us who sin. This is why it is so important for us to forgive and repent to God, because we sin and die daily.

"Spiritual wickedness in high places," the wickedness in high places.

> Wherein time past ye walked according to
> the course of this world, according to the prince
> of the power of the air, the spirit that now work
> in the children of disobedience. (Ephesians 2:2)

After breaking down the scripture Ephesians 6:12, we can get back to our topic on spiritual rape and the dealings of the human spirits in chapter 2.

CHAPTER 2

The Human Spirit

The human spirit is dead to God, because of our trespasses to sins. If the Spirit does not go where you command it to go, then you are dealing with the human spirit. When you are being attacked by a human spirit, it can weaken your faith because you believe that it is an evil spirit and it should be cast out in Jesus's name, that's why it's so important to determine your attacker. The human spirit can attack a person physically, mentally, emotionally, and spiritually. The devil can come in and attack you when you're sinning and keep living in sin, until a person turns from their sins and when they do, that's when the devil feels like he's losing his hold on us. He begins to attack our life; he does not bother the people living a life full of sin because he feels he already has them.

In the book of Ephesians, God tells us to put on the whole armor of God.

> Finally my brethren be strong in the power
> of his might, put on the whole armor of God,
> that ye may be able to stand against the wiles of
> the devil. (Ephesians 6:10–11)

The word "wiles" means to trick, intended to deceive or ensnare, disarming, or seductive manner that is meant to fool, trap, or entice, or deceitful, cunning, and trickery. Wiles are the evil things done in our lives by the devil, who is attacking us physically, mentally, emotionally, and spiritually, and only God can heal us. Only God can restore us, especially if we have been abused physically, emotionally, spiritually, and sexually. The only way we can be restored is to humble our hearts to God, so he can heal us completely.

In the beginning, the serpent (the devil) deceived Eve into eating from the tree, which God had forbidden Adam to eat from. The devil tricked Eve by telling her that her eyes would be opened and she surely wouldn't die. Read chapter 3 in the book of Genesis. We will continue to speak on spiritual rape and spiritual abuse throughout this book, because we must get a clear understanding of what we are dealing with, wickedness in high places, principalities, powers, and rulers of darkness of this world. The devil is trying to gather up as many people as he can to build up a kingdom of his own, but he knows his time in limited on this Earth. Time is running out, people of God. The only way God is going to heal this wicked world is if we do as he said,

> If my people who are called by my name would humble themselves, and pray, seek my face, and turn from their wicked ways, then we will hear from heaven and I will forgive them of their sins and will heal the land. (2 Chronicles 7:14)

If we continue to live the world's way, then we will see more evil in the land, so we are still dealing with the human spirit. The human spirit is the very breath of the almighty God for God breathed into man his spirit. "And God said, Let us make man in our own image, after our likeness" (Genesis 1:26). So God breathed the breath of life into Adam and God made man by breathing his spirit into man, who possesses the human spirits. The human spirit has a spirit that does not sleep, it is a very powerful spirit, and every human has its own spirit. The human spirit is composed of six elements, which forms a different world. The spirit world influences every human being, but the soul is slightly different from the earthly body. The soul contains the true spirit with the spiritual mind. The true spirit is the spiritual mind and soul.

In order for *us* to understand about spiritual abuse, we must also understand about the human spirit and the functions of our spirit. We must believe God himself, but we must understand how to connect with God spiritually. Our soul is basically who we are our, our mind, our emotions, and our will. The function of our soul is to express ourselves to God. Some of our thoughts are our own and some are God's. We must personally experience in discerning God's thoughts, repent, and invite God to use us, then we will hear from God. Wait on God to confirm his will for your life, you will hear from God like Mary did (Luke 1:46–47). Mary's soul magnified the Lord. She lived and worshipped God in her spirit, which directed her soul, her praise to God from her spirit was expressed through her soul.

There is a war going on in the mind. God wants your mind and the devil wants your mind, but you must fight off all negative thoughts that come into your mind. It's the devil that's trying to put evil thoughts in your mind. The invisible war refers to the soul and mind, the spiritual realm (Ephesians 6:12, Hebrews 11:3). What is required for us to believe, we must believe in the physical realm to be welcomed into God's presence, his spiritual realm. There have been some people who were able to see with their physical eyes in the spiritual realm, the invisible realm (Daniel 10:7–17, 2 Kings 6:11–17). God allowed them to bridge the gap in the physical realm to see into the spiritual realm. God opened the eyes of Elisha's servant to see the host of God's army. His spiritual eyes were opened to see the spiritual warfare going on around him, and only Daniel saw the angels standing before him, everyone else felt the terror and fled. Daniel was granted access to see, hear, and speak spiritually as he communicated with the angels. The Lord is with us and he will provide for us through his angels. God has chosen to love and protect us physically as he works things out for us spiritually, we are learning about the spiritual realm. These invisible or unseen forces are real. Job is a perfect example of a spiritual conflict. The devil wanted to destroy and kill Job, but the devil asked for God's permission before he could even touch Job. The spiritual conflict was manifested in the physical form, Job's life into the spiritual realm. Job was a righteous man, who stood upright before God. Job was a man after God's own heart.

CHAPTER 3

The Functions of the Spirit, Body, and Soul

The Spirit, Body, and Soul and Its Functions

The functions of the soul, the spirit, and the body diagram: the spirit is the inner layer, the soul is in the middle, and the body is the outer layer. The body is the world consciousness, the soul is the self-consciousness, and the spirit is the God consciousness. There are five organs in the body, which are your five senses, the five senses dwell in the body. God dwells in the spirit, the spirit works with the soul to communicate to the body (man). This is the way man is able to worship and communicate with God. The soul is the meeting place where the body and the spirit connects, man communicates with God's spirit in the spiritual realm. The spirit controls the body, the soul is in between the two. The soul binds the spirit and the body together as one. The spirit can control the body through the soul, causing it to submit unto God. The brain and the heart functions come from the soul, and the body and the soul are controlled by the spirit of God.

When people are living according to the word of God (Bible), those who fear God stay away from doing evil. The human spirit struggles to understand because the fleshly body tries to take over when evil spirits are present. The human spirit can be used with the same meaning as the human soul. The human spirit is sometimes used to impersonate the human soul. The soul is located in between the heart and the brain; only the other parts of the body will become dead and feel nothing, because the soul keeps the heart and the brain alive. The human body is made up of five elements: water, air, heat, and dust, and (intelligence) space. The spirit communicates with God. The human spirit is the very breath of God as he breathed into man the breath of life in the beginning of the creation.

The human spirit is what gives us consciousness of self, and limited qualities like God, so we must not allow self to limit us from God's will for our lives. The human spirit includes our intelligence, emotions, passions, and fears. The human spirit provides us the ability to comprehend and understand (Job 33:14). The unseen human spirit governs man's mental and emotional existence. Every human being has a spirit, but the human spirit was damaged in the fall when Adam sinned and his ability to fellowship with God was broken. He did not die physically that day, but he died spiritually (Acts 2:38). Adams was made alive by the breath of God, the Holy Spirit (Holy Ghost). We are new creations in Christ Jesus. We are made alive, spiritually alive, by the breath of God, the Holy Spirit. As God's children, we are no longer led by our own spirit, but by God's spirits and if we follow the Holy Spirit, it will lead us into eternal life. The true spirit of a human is a fragment of God's energy located in the solar plexus, it is composed of pure godlike spiritual energy unlike any other form of energy. The soul is a form of physical existence, it is the fourth dimension (ethereal). The physical body of any human being in order to understand these things you must look up the seven main chakras as it will explain how energy flows and works in the body. The soul is slightly different from the earthly body. The soul contains the true spirit a spiritual mind and soul.

People who are religious will debate with a person over the truth that's in the Bible. Most people do not know that they are defending the world's view instead of God's word. "Repent for the kingdom of heaven is at hand" (Matthews 4:17). We live in a very wicked world, but thanks to God, we have his promises and his word will not return back to him void. We must read God's word to get a better understanding of his knowledge of who he is and about his spirit that lives inside of us. We must tap into the spiritual realm of God.

CHAPTER 4

Spiritual Husband and Wife

The Spiritual Husband and Wife is a spirit of Satan, a demon you cannot see with your natural eyes, but you can see them spiritually in your dreams and visions. These evil spirits (demons) are as real as humans. An Incubus male, a sexual demon or evil spirit that has sexual intercourse with a woman while she's asleep, is called a Spiritual Husband. A Succubus, a female sexual demon which has sexual intercourse with a man while he is asleep, is called a Spiritual Wife. These spirits are summoned by Satan to destroy Christians, believers, homes, and relationships. These demons are sleeping with human beings. These spirits are very dangerous. They will kill and steal, your joy, your peace, and even mess with your health. They will affect your brain, your calling, your virtue. The Spiritual Husband and Wife will destroy your marriage or your human partner's life. All these Spirits need is an open door. These demons can enter in and manifest by pornography, perverse sexual activity, and immortality.

A Spiritual Husband and Wife can be inherited through generational curses, through the bloodline curses, these evil spirits can cause destruction on a person or individual through tattooing and incisions. These demons feed off your sexual energy, they will lie upon you while you're sleeping.

I want to briefly talk about empathy. This will lead us into a different form of spiritual rape.

Pulling on the Spirit

God has given some of us the Gift of Empathy, which is the capacity to feel and understand what another person is experiencing from within. God also has giving some people the capability to place oneself in another's shoes. Empathy will give a person the feelings that you are understanding and sharing another person's experiences and emotions. This gift will give you the ability to share someone else's feelings, most prophets have this Gift of Empathy and this is a gift from God, which is called Mirror Neurons. When you react to emotions, expressed by others and allow you the ability to reproduce these feelings. Neurons are remarkable cells that form human empathy because a person can transport into another person's mind briefly, making a person feel what someone else is feeling.

Now, we are going to deal with spiritual rape in a different form. The natural body and the spiritual body—the human spirit that leaves the body and travels into the heaven, the first heaven is the atmosphere, which contains the stars and the moon. The second heaven contains angels and demons, and the third heaven, is where a person spirit leaves their body, which is called an outer body experience. The human spirit can violate another person's or violate the privacy of an individual, which brings us to astral travelers or spiritual travelers, that taps into the planes and travel into planes. The astral plane is the unseen by the physical eyes, but we know that they exist. Spiritual rape is another form done while sleeping, it's not of God.

Now let's deal with these demons that attacks a person while they are sleeping. The Succubus and Incubus, these demons have sexual intercourse with a person while they are asleep—Spiritual Rape. Falling angels who decided to follow Satan rather than God. The Bible called them begotten giants, evil spirits that wishes to defile our temple that belongs to God (Genesis 6:24). Nephilim, or falling angel, are spirits that Satan uses as spiritual weapons, unseen battles in the second heaven (Acts 19:13–17). It is illegal for demons and angels to marry.

Noah and the Fall of Man

In the Bible, the story of Noah, during this time, God told Noah to build and ark because during this time the fallen angels, the begotten giants, had started having sexual intercourse with the women. The fallen angels were taking human wives for themselves, teaching them how to make things and they started having children with the humans and they bore giants, and wickedness was in the world. Story is found in Genesis 6:1–8. This is where human beings began to increase in numbers on the earth and the daughters were born to them. The sons of God saw the daughters of humans were beautiful and they took them as wives and killing the ones that had husbands. Then the Lord said, "My spirit will not contend with humans forever, for they are now mortal, their days will be a hundred and twenty years. The Nephilim spirits was upon the Earth in these days and also afterward, when the sons of God went to the daughters of human and had children by them. They were the heroes of old, men of renown. The Lord saw how wicked the human race had become on earth, and every inclination of the thought of the human heart was evil at all times. The Lord regretted that he had made (us) human beings, and his heart was deeply troubled, so the Lord said he will wipe from the face of the earth the human race. I have created and I will also destroy with them all the animals, the birds, and every living creature that moves along the ground, for I regret the day I have made them but Noah found favor in eyes of the Lord. You will have to continue reading the rest of the story of Noah in the Bible, I was only given a brief summary of the story.

The Curse of the Spiritual Husband and Wife

This is a curse. A spiritual husband and wife are demons, evil spirits. How to know if you have this type of spirit that is having sex in your dreams, deprives the marital partner sex, and will steal their affection, and attack your husband or wife? These spirits will make you start hating your spouse, which will lead to sexual immorality. Masturbation is a sex demon, homosexual thoughts demons, prostitution demons, barrenness and low sperm count. When they are having sex with a person in a dream, they are defiling a person and stealing what's theirs, giving diseases and sickness. A Spiritual Husband and Wife goes hand in hand with Jezebel. We must ask God to deliver us from the Spiritual Husband and Wife in Jesus's name. Repent of your sins and the sins of your forefathers. Ask the Lord to deliver oneself in Jesus's name if you expect that you are in bondage. But if you do not accept that you are in bondage, you will stay in bondage and the Spiritual Husband or Wife will destroy your marriage or you may never get married. This spirit will kill you and take you to hell with them. Repent for the kingdom of God is at hand. Repent, repent, and repent.

CHAPTER 5

Emotional Rape

What is Emotional Rape?

Emotional rape is similar to physical rape or date rape, which involves the sexual use of someone's body without their consent. Emotional rape is the use of someone's emotions such as love without consent. Emotional rape is common, but not limited to male or female relationship. People who have been emotionally raped can be both man and woman, in which both forms of rape can be very damaging to a person's spirit, it will cause a person not to trust or love anybody ever again. This is very dangerous for a person's mental health and if they do not let go or be healed from this they might be scarred for life.

Emotional manipulation and abuse will hold you psychologically bond. This person will use their powers to control or lure you into getting what they want, such as sex, money, or will try to destroy a person emotionally, physically, psychologically, mentally, and spiritually in the process. Scriptures to read on the pain of sexual abuse are Isaiah 53:5, Psalms 34:17–20, 1 Peter 3:7. On emotional abuse, read Ephesians 6:4, 4:2, Psalms 34:17–20, Romans 8:1.

Sexual rape is to violate someone's body. Emotional rape is the violation of the human soul, which will lead to trust issues. Date rape is to violate someone's body without consent or knowledge. Trust issues with emotional rape, when people have been hurt by others, their wounds are so deep within the soul because that person they loved and respect has raped their soul. Soul rape will cause a person to struggle with self-hatred or self-loathing and it will also cause a person to dislike or hate themselves. They will always be angry with themselves or their family.

Self-Hatred

Self-hatred will cause you to blame others or will be very shameful. This causes that person to start judging in their own mind and spirit that it will involve the soul. We are born sinful since the fall of Adam and Eve. Wherefore as by one man sin entered into the world, and death by sin and so death passed upon all men, for that all have sinned (Romans 5:12). Once we were dead because of our disobedience and our many sins (Ephesians 2:1).

We, as believers, uses to live in sin just like the rest of the world, obeying the devil who is the commander of the power in the unseen world. The devil is at work in the hearts and minds of those who refuse to obey God. God loves us so much that even in our sins, he gave us life when he raised his only begotten son Jesus Christ from the dead. God had a plan for us since the beginning of time. God's plan for us didn't include us living in the sins of our past, God wants us to have a relationship with him. God intended for us to enjoy his love and energy being in his presence, he wants us to be healed and free from all sin. We have an image of God based on our pain and images of those that are in authority. The book of Ephesians is a letter showing us his love for us from the beginning of time. God will continue to love us no matter what we do, his love for us is unconditional. Only through God's son Jesus Christ can we be saved. Jesus died that we might have life (Ephesians Chapter 1).

CHAPTER 6

Narcissism

Warning signs of a spiritual narcissist can be corrupt leaders always wanting credit for everything, always saying, "I, I, I, me, me, me." We are born with sinful tendencies and are not righteous (Galatians 5:19–21). The flesh is a part of our sinful nature. Totally focusing on oneself is called egocentrism. It also means a person that is an adult but the mind is still childlike and it's hard for this person to grow up or have a relationship. Even though egocentrism and narcissism appear to be similar, they are not the same.

Narcissism is a condition that ranges from normal behavior to pathological behavior. Narcissism is used by psychologists to define a person as being pre-occupied with one's self. It's a very selfish person that dominates or engrosses the mind of someone to absorb in someone's own thoughts. Pride with sin (Proverbs 16:18). A narcissistic person will idealize him or herself so that they will not have to deal with their own mistakes or sins, they are non-empathetic, haughty, envious, manipulative, and have a sense of entitlement. Pride will make them believe that they have a good heart and will not allow them to see their own sins, and they will cover them up. Most narcissists are very dangerous people because they will try and destroy a person or get someone else to destroy that person if they cannot control them.

We are slaves to our body (flesh) (Romans 7:5). God tells us in his word that we must love others, we must think of others, unseen of our own self. A narcissistic person does not do well with authorities and has a hard time loving others. They will hurt everyone that is close to them without feeling any remorse. This is a part of our sinful nature that we are sometimes not aware that exist within us (people). In 2 Timothy 3:1–7, Paul told them to watch out for what feeds the behavior of people, whether it is love or money, for their image, self-love, and attitude. Some leaders may have that type of behavior. Sometimes they will portray an image of having money and power. They love attention, always seeking love, and feels like no one has or will ever love them. They boast all the time, their whole conversation is about "me, me, me and I, I, I." They talk about themselves at all times. They are considered to be very evil and dangerous.

Evil is at work in the unseen world and is at work in people's bodies and minds, so we must be careful not to allow this spirit to take over and dwell in us. Abuse of evil is in our government, politicians, and religion. This can lead people to believe evil is the abuse of power and it is power that is used in the unseen world, as well as in this world. The devil uses his abuse of evil by trying to control our bodies and mind, he tries to find a body to use, and evil spirits can only enter the body through sin (John 10:1–10). Satan tries to use his powers to destroy us.

The Bible tells us that the devil comes to kill, steal, and destroy, but God comes that we might have life and it more abundantly (Ephesians 6:10–11). We are not wrestling with flesh and blood, we are dealing with evil spirits that want to take over our minds and control us because an evil spirit needs a way to enter the body. This is why the Bible tells us to put on the whole armor of God because physically and mentally we must cover· our head (mind). The devil can enter into the body and mind of a person, he really wants the mind because if he controls the mind he can cause a person to not be in control. Emotionally and spiritually, we must guard our heart and soul. The devil can enter in a person's heart if they hold *unforgiveness* in it. We leave an open door for the enemy to enter in. So please put on the whole armor of God so our body is guarded.

CHAPTER 7

Pulpit Rape

Spiritual rape and soul rape results to having a tortured soul (Psalms 147:3). Religious persecution is abuse, mishandling a person or a group of people based upon a spiritual affiliation or belief. When innocent souls trust those that are in authority for protection, only to be used, and manipulated or betrayed is also a form of rape. Spiritual rape or spiritual abuse violates the soul. Religious abuse, especially when they are close to you, will leave a person hurt and scarred. A person destroys the most intimate aspect of a person's existence, which only God can restore.

I mentioned earlier in the book that God will have to restore a person physically, mentally, emotionally, and spiritually, and so people have to be restored sexually too because of the things that are done by leadership or relationships. Pulpit rape is done by a leader who controls the thoughts of others and their behavior while doing it in the name of God, and using it as an instrument of violence too. Misrepresent God by hurting the innocents created in God's own image is also pulpit rape.

A spiritual abuser uses mind control that runs deep. Its instruments are the hands of authority who uses good people for their own selfish purposes and reasons (Colossians 2:1). The people who bear the rape of the soul have wounds so deep, pain so great that it affects the core of their being, which is created in the image of God. There is something so wrong about having your genuine love for God to be used to destroy your spirit, especially children, because they trust naturally and are pure. God wants our relationship with him to be pure like a little child, so we can simply trust him, any other kind of faith is not appropriate and un-natural. If a person is unable to trust, it will consume them and it will take God to heal them. God will have to heal them before they can move forward.

Church Hurt

Are you not concerned about the needs of the people or their souls? Church hurt can be hard to see at first if you have never encountered it before. In most churches where the leaders or pastors are very manipulative and want the church people to follow them, unsteady of following God, and allowing the Holy Spirit to lead them. People who are under a controlling leader who will tell a person they cannot leave the church, or if they leave the church they will not be blessed, or they will cause a curse to come upon themselves if they leave. That's a lie from the pit of hell. These leaders that do this are operating under the spirit of control, by using fear to control people by saying that they will no longer be under God's protection (John 4:18). Controlling leaders control the people in the church into fear so that they can build their religious kingdom. We are supposed to build up God's kingdom on love, by teaching the people in the church about God's love and they will be able to go out in the world and teach others and bring them to God. Most leaders that are controlling are focused on their own personal needs being met and are not concerned about the needs of the people or their souls (Matthews 23:4). These are the things that Pharisees did to control the people. We call the Pharisees of today spiritual leaders who are manipulative and controlling in the pulpit, and it is pulpit rape (Jude 1:11).

Church hurt comes in because of the leaders raping the people over the pulpit, taking their money, convincing them to give, controlling the thoughts and emotions of the people, and they are not getting healed. How does a person walk into a church and walk back out still sick, hurt, and abused? We walk in a church where it is supposed to be like a hospital for healing God's people, but because the people in the church are only concerned about what you're wearing or how much money you can give, or the leaders are only preaching on prosperity, instead of preaching God's truth and healing. If you are worried about money and material things, then a person cannot worry about the things of God. When we worry about money or material things, and fame or fortune, we cannot get healed. We must focus on the things of God. In order to be healed, we must have faith and believe that God will heal us.

God shares in our emotions (Psalms 33:15). God knows our weaknesses (Hebrews 4:15, Romans 8:26). God feels our pain. We have emotions because we are made in God's image. He understands our pain. He suffered also the same pain. Jesus had been betrayed, abandoned, fatigued. Jesus came to this world and lived as a human. He experienced everything that we as human beings have experienced. God understands our pain. Jesus understands our weaknesses. The Holy Spirit understands our feelings. The moment we get tired, the Holy Spirit does our praying for us when we do not know what to pray for. The Bible says when we are in pain, the Holy Spirit prays for us, making prayers out of our wordless pain and tears. The Holy Spirit knows our feelings. If you're hurting, you do not have to go through it alone. Jesus left with us a comforter—the Holy Spirit, the spirit of truth—to intercede on our behalf (John14:7).,

God will never leave us alone to deal with our own pain. We must give everything to God. We must allow God to meet our spiritual needs and the only things God desires from us is to seek him not man. We live in a world that is conflicting, with confusing beliefs, full of problems, and with serious spiritual needs. The gift of God shall lead us into repentance. We must humble ourselves, fall on our knees, and call upon his name, giving God the glory and thanking him for our many blessings. Asking God to heal us from the hurt of others and to please forgive them so that we may be healed, and be free from pulpit rape, the church hurt, and allow our soul to heal, in Jesus's name. Amen.

CHAPTER 8

Unclean Spirits

Demons are unclean spirits, which are wicked. These demons try to attack the human body because in order to operate they need a body to use. Unclean spirits come to destroy all God's creations. When these unclean spirits (demons) begin to take over a person's body, they try to defile the body and control the mind with evil thoughts. Most people also think that fallen angels are evil spirits, so fallen angels must also have a body to use. For a body without the Spirit is dead (James 2:26) so faith without works is dead also. A spirit can live without a body, but a body cannot live without a spirit.

Unclean spirits mean time defiled, fixity, dirty, foul persons that seem clean on the outside but are foul and dirty on the inside. These persons will always think filthy dirty thoughts and these spirits that dwell enjoy the company of others with the same unclean spirits. He that hath no rule over his own spirit is like a city that is broken down and without walls (Proverbs 25:23). Unclean spirits come to destroy all of God's creations. When these demons begin to take over a persons body to defile it by trying to control the mind with evil thoughts, causing your mind, heart, and soul to weaken your spirit that you will lose your faith. These unclean spirits will try and make you think you are mentally unstable, and once in the mind, these spirits begin to attack your body causing physical illness. Do not give into these evil thoughts. We must stay in God's word. We must study and hide God's word in our heart and continue to pray. Evil spirits will suppress someone in their sleep. We must pray that the Holy Spirit strikes all evil spirits while a person is sleeping in the name of Jesus.

"To deliver such an one unto Satan for the destruction of the flesh that the Spirit maybe saved in the day of the Lord Jesus" (1 Corinthians 5:5). Defilement comes from within our heart so God works his healing from the inside out. We are defiled by what we say.

> Then Jesus called to the crowd to come and hear, all of you listen, and he said and try to understand. You are not defiled by what you eat, you are defiled by what you say and do. (Mark7:14–15)

> And then he added it is the thought life that defines you, for from within or without of a person's heart comes evil thoughts, sexual immorality, theft, murder. Adultery, greed, wickedness, deceit, eagerness for lustful pleasure, envy, slander, pride, and foolishness. All these things come from within, and defile the man. (Mark 7:20–23)

They are what defines you and make you unacceptable to God. Our thoughts can become an extension of our soul. How are our thoughts and extension to our soul? Because our thoughts create our reality, it can be difficult for a person to come to terms with what they're thinking—the thoughts that live inside our head. The mind is very powerful, but we must not allow our thoughts to control our mind because sometimes our thoughts are evil. We also must not dwell on our mistakes or allow our minds to keep on thinking bad thoughts because this allows evil spirits to come in and take over our mind. That's what the devil does. It tries and places evil thoughts in our mind to control us so we must try and think positive. Thinking positive can block out evil thoughts or bad behavior. A double minded man is unstable in all thy ways (James 2:8).

CHAPTER 9

Mental Illness

The mind, will, emotions, and spirit of a man. The Bible speaks the difference between the physically sick or mentally sick (mental illness, paralysis, and demonic possession). Evil spirits try to destroy the mind by torturing a person. Where did demons come from? (Matthews 8:28–32). Evil spirits are enemies of mankind during Moses's time. They are spiritual adversaries that mislead and destroy mankind. Demons enter human bodies without permission. Demons possess people's minds which cause them to suffer from mental illness. The Bible called people that we call mentally ill or possessed, blind, deaf, dumb, mute, or mean, all evil spirits. Diverse diseases or tormented are those which were possessed with demons and those which were called lunatics, and palsy (Matthew 4:24). Sick—Kakos—sick, ill. Diseases—nosos—disease, infirmity sickness. Torments—basanos—tortured physically or mentally—posso seed with demons (daimon Romel) under the power of evil spirits. Lumtic-seleniazonal which means controlled people with epilepsy. Palsy—paraleotikos—paralyzed.

Biblical Counselors

How does Psychology work with biblical counseling? Biblical counselors where man is basically trying to deal with spiritual nature. Psychology is the study of the mind and human and abnormal behavior of everyday living. Psychology is man's attempt to understand the spiritual side and to repair the spiritual side of man without reference or recognition of the spirit of God and his word. The Bible states that mankind is a unique creation of God. The Bible also deals with man's spirituality, and the fall of man into sin, and man's relationship with God (Ephesians 2:1, Genesis 2:7, 1:26). God is the source of understanding and knowledge. He is the one who created the mind. So in order to understand the mind, you must understand who God is and his spirit. The one who created mankind, the mind, and human behavior.

A lot of people are in the hospital not because of physical illness, but because of emotional, mental, and psychological problems. Read the books of Samuel (1, 2) and Kings (1, 2). A psychologically unstable person is dealing with problems of the soul. Sin is basically the problems for all illnesses of the body, mind, and soul. Sin channels sickness in the body. Abnormal thoughts and behavior, madness or insanity, and mental illness were clearly known throughout the Bible. Jesus was thought to be insane by his family (Mark 3:21, John 10:20–26). Jesus healed lunatics (Matthew 17:15), Paul is mad (Acts 26:24–25). Believers could be thought of as being mad (Corinthians 11:23). Abnormal thoughts and behavior, and mental illnesses were dearly known throughout the Bible history. The Bible states mental illness in references regarding madness and insanity (Deuteronomy 28:28, 1 Samuel 21:13–15). Madness compared to foolish behavior (Proverbs 26:18). Madness is the opposite of wisdom. Madness and insanity describe a set of thoughts and behavior. Mental illness refers to madness and insanity in the Bible (1 Samuel 21:13–15). Prophets and servants thought to be mad (2 Kings 9:11). Madness compared to foolish behavior (Proverbs 26:18). Madness is the opposite of wisdom. Bipolar disorder or manic depression (John 10:10, 17:17, 15:22; and James 2:1). Deep emotional problems, self-love. The Bible commands us to love ourselves. We cannot love God and others until we love ourselves first (Ephesians 5:28–29, Philippians 2:3, Mark 8:35).

Can sin be called a disorder? Yes, not being right with God can be a result. When you have the peace of God, which passes all understanding, you will not sin. Yes, sin can be called a disorder. Bipolar disorder, is a bio-chemical disease or genetic disease that affects one of the biochemical processes in the human body, which sometimes cause mental illness, and these illnesses are caused by sin. When emotionally ill, faith and hope and gone.

Bipolar Disorders

These disorders involve the brain, and sin can make you physically sick, you can suffer depression and anxiety. (The word says be anxious for nothing.) Stress can cause a heart attack. It weakens the immune system. Once your immune system is weakened, it can cause a number of diseases.

The Bible states that depression, anxiety, insanity, paranoia, and stress, all are caused by living a sinful life (Psalms 38:1–5, 9, 17–18, Psalms 69:20, Proverbs 4:18–19, Jeremiah 17:9, Mark 2:17, Romans 1:27). Disorders are still a sin. God deals with the mind and so does Satan. Satan tries to play with your mind by trying to put evil thoughts there. God has given us free will that lets us choose to serve either heaven or hell, so we are responsible for our own actions. Choose this day whom you're going to serve, life or death.

CHAPTER 10

Jezebel Spirit

Queen Jezebel

In the Old Testament, Jezebel was a wicked queen. She married King Ahab, who believed in God. Jezebel was a false prophetess who worshipped the god of Baal. Jezebel was a witch and her spirit of witchcraft and warlock spirit is still operating today in the church all over the world. Jezebel and King Ahab had three children, two sons named Ahaziah and Jehoram, and one daughter named Athaliah, who also was evil, the daughter from hell. Jezebel's spirit is sociopathic. She gains power by destroying others with her manipulating and controlling spirit. There was a three-fold demonic cord with Jezebel, her daughter Ahaziah, and Delilah. You can read about Delilah in the book of Judges Chapter 16, the story of Samson and Delilah. These ladies would go after your now, your future to try and take after your way, your promises, your call that God has placed on your very life. Jezebel has the nastiest evil, most disgusting, cunning, seductive spirit in Satan's kingdom. These spirits have been known for taking down pastors, prophets, and ministers (churches) and destroying companies, friendships, and marriages. These spirits will cause people to commit suicide and even murder. The different kind of demonic spirits, they have their names created and given by God. They have a functional name that tells what type of spirits you're dealing with. For example, lust, anger, murder. I will give all of these spirits later. There are levels of wickedness in Satan's (the devil's) kingdom (Matthew 12:43). These spirits operate the same way every time, intelligent, cunning, and seductive spirits. These spirits love to break up good and godly relationships.

Jesus called a woman who called herself Prophetess Jezebel, who was teaching God's people to commit fornication and to eat meat that was offered to idols. These are the different types of spirits Jezebel has: witchcraft and warlock spirit—demonic spirits, greed, pride, lust, jealousy, envy, strife, anger, bitterness, and rebellion. All these spirits fight and battle each other for first place inside of human beings. These spirits will cause a person to lose their mind or become confused and have no control anymore (Peter 5:8, Matthew 12:43). Jezebel knows scriptures. She knows how to talk to gain favor with leaders then once she gets close and think she has them, she sets out to destroy them. Jezebel has the spirit to draw people. These demons act very spiritual and a person will think she has a very close spiritual walk with God but she doesn't. Jezebel seduces a person until she has them. This seducing spirit alone will take a person over. This is how she is able to take over a church, leaders, and marriages, and destroys them or even kills them. Remember the devil comes to steal, kill, and destroy with that witchcraft and warlock spirit.

The different type of spirits Jezebel operates in are pride, lust, seductive, vile, hate, false prophecies and visions, dreams, self-centered, always wanting to be the center of attention, narcissistic, judgmental, demanding, critical, cunning, cold-hearted, ruthless, calculating, combative, lying, cheating, confrontational, do not like constructive criticism, manipulating, demeaning. Jezebel hated all prophets. Jezebel hates prayer, hates spiritual warfare, and always operates in the witchcraft or warlock spirit and sometimes works in both witchcraft and warlock spirits. Jezebel loves people that are in power or that are very intelligent and nice-looking, like most leaders. Jezebel loves to play mind games, getting to know a person's weaknesses, she/he will always attack your weak points to begin to destroy a person. Jezebel will come after your calling that God has placed on your life. She/he will try and destroy your self-esteem and confidence. Jezebel will try to make a person go crazy. She/he will have you thinking that she/he has all the wisdom and knowledge. Jezebel wants a person to totally depend on her/him. Jezebel will try to bring a person down so that they will become depressed and confused. Jezebel will try to suck the very life out of a person, by taking them down piece by piece, so a person can no longer walk in their calling for God. Jezebel tries to destroy your faith. Jezebel had the Prophet Elijah so depressed and confused, he wanted God to take his life, but God used an angel to bring him food as he was hiding in a cave so he could eat and become strong enough to give his a word to carry out to Ahab. Jezebel had set out to kill Elijah and all prophets of God or any one that came up against her or her husband King Ahab. Jezebel will go to any lengths to destroy the calling on a person's life. She will work on making a lot of illnesses to come up on a person's body. She will play with a person's mind until they even want to commit suicide. Remember, if Jezebel could kill prophets and have Elijah running for his life, we are no match for Jezebel. Remember, she will go after anyone in leadership positions, which include pastors, ministers, prayer groups, worship leaders, husbands, wives, companies, and businesses. So if you think that Jezebel's spirit is operating in your life you must let go of your pride.

There are six things that the Lord hates and seven that are detestable to him (Proverbs 6:16–19). Haughty eyes and a lying tongue, hands that shed innocent blood, a heart that devises wicked schemes, feet that are quick to push into evil, a false witness who pours out lies, and a person who stirs up conflict in the community or that sows discord among the brethren. Jezebel operates in all these things God detests. So if you feel like these spirits are trying to control you, repent and ask God the purpose for all the turmoil that is in your life. Rebuke the devil and ask God to give you strength. Pray, pray, pray.

In the next chapter on spiritual warfare, it will teach you how to wage war against these evil spirits, so you can be delivered from all evil spirits. Jezebel was order to be killed by Jehu, who ordered her to be pushed out of a window to her death, and he ordered the servants to go bury her. But when they went to go bury Jezebel body it was eaten up and scattered by dogs, just like it was predicted by the prophets. It was prophesied that the dogs would eat up her flesh and scatter her bones. Elijah killed 450 plus 400 of Jezebel's prophets.

God told Elijah that he would raise up seven thousand prophets who have not bowed down to Baal (1 Kings 19:16–18).

Even though Queen Jezebel is dead, those evil spirits are still on earth today. We must be aware of these spirits and learn how to destroy these spirits off our lives, which brings us to the next chapter on spiritual warfare.

CHAPTER II

Spiritual Warfare

The battle we are not fighting against human beings, but against the wicked spiritual forces in the heavenly world, the rulers, and the power of the dark ages (Ephesians 6:12). There's an unseen battle going on in the spirit realm, which we don't feel but is happening. A spiritual warfare in the dimensions between God and Satan, between good and evil, between angels and demons. We are caught right in the middle and Satan wants to destroy us, the people of God (Ephesians 6:12). There is a spiritual warfare going on for our prayers, Satan throws darts at a person while they are waiting on God to answer our prayers. He sends things to block our prayers. Like depression, Satan tries to disappoint and discourages us while we wait for God to answer. Satan throws darts of delay (Daniel 10:12–13). There's always a battle going on over our prayers, delayed but not denied. The Holy Spirit is fighting for us, so hold on, be strong, and don't give up, stand. The Spirit of God moves upon the earth. Sometimes God allows evil spirits to come and low stress us for a certain purpose, more than one spirit can possess a body (1 Timothy 4:1).

The Battles We Battle

Now the Holy Spirit tells us clearly that in the last days some people will turn away from the truth (faith). They will follow deceptive spirits and false teachings that come from demons, evil spirits. Verses on false teaching: Ezekiel 13:9, 1 John 4:1–6, Mathew 7:15–20, 2 Peter 2, Mathew 24:24, 2 Timothy 4:3–4, Matthew 23:1–29.

Spiritual Warfare

Spiritual Warfare is the concept of fighting against the works of unearthly evil forces that is based on the biblical beliefs in evil spirits or demons that are said to intervene in human affairs in varies ways (Wikipedia). The children of Israel was in bondage. A person will never change their mindset or change the condition of their living in order to change their life. There is a spiritual battle going on in the earth where demons and evil spirits are released upon the earth to destroy the people of God. We must prepare for warfare of body and flesh. God has given us a human spirit with free will. The Holy Spirit dwells within your soul, which belongs to God—the spirit that we deal with. God has given us free will to serve him, so choose this day who you're going to serve.

The Worldly Battle

We battle with living in sin, struggling with loving the things of this world, it is when we come out of sin, and a person will begin to battle with the things that kept them in sin. God said, "Come from among them" (the world). "Therefore come out from among them and be ye separate," said the Lord, "and touch not the unclean things, and I will receive you" (2 Corinthians 6:17).

The Battle within Us

Battling within, we deal with mind control, the struggle with letting things go, holding on to past hurt, unforgiveness, brokenness from relationships, rejections, and abuse (2 Corinthians 10:3–5, Revelation 12:7–9, 1 John 5:4–5, Romans 6:1–23).

Being Balanced and Unbalanced

What does the Bible says about being balanced? Being level headed (1 Timothy 6:17). Believers should be balanced in your everyday life. We can live a balanced life by totally surrendering our lives over to God. We can balance our lives by living and enjoying God's blessings. The fruits of the spirit are love, joy, peace, kindness, goodness, faithfulness, gentleness, and self-control (Galatians 5:22–24). We must not place anything above worshiping God (2 Samuel 13:1–22). We must not worship anything worldly because it will cause a person to be unbalanced and will lead to sin. We must not worship idols, such as sources, houses, cars, material things, relationships, *etc.*, because God is a jealous God. The First Commandment is to love the Lord God with all thy might (Luke 14:26). The only way to be balanced in your life is to be free from sin and temptation in this world. We must totally give our lives over to God. Seeking his purpose for our life and follow his Commandments. Read the book of Proverbs, it's the book of instructions on how we are supposed to live our lives, how to raise our customers, families, and run our household. Is living unbalanced a sin? Being unbalanced is a sin (Proverbs 11:1). A false balance is an abomination to the Lord, but a just weight is God's delight. Address false balance in order to balance your life in God. Read God's word, live according to his word, repent and turn from sin (wrongdoing), and turn to God. "And it shall come to pass that whosoever shall call upon the name of the Lord shall be saved" (Acts 2:31).

The Bible states that you have angels you *can* call upon that are really placed in your life to help you fight battles. Angels can come to a person's aid to block and attack, but you must believe and pray to God for protection since everybody is being attacked spiritually. We must strengthen our spirit by studying the word of God.

Spiritual Sex Demons and Sex Spirits

Struggling with someone else's sins, the things that a person must do is get sin out of their life, if you don't have sin in your life you may be carrying someone else's sins. We sometimes can experience dealing with sins of others because a person maybe lusting after another person. This is called Sex Spirits, which is when someone has an attraction that's spiritual not physical, and most of the times, leaders fall because of this spiritual attraction that that someone has for them. This person can have dreams about them and are not even aware of what's going on or what a person is doing. Sometimes this will happen if a person is lusting after another person or fantasizing in their sleep about that person. It brings on these spirits of sex demons. The reason why I'm talking about these sexual spirits is because a lot of pastors and leaders struggle with this type of demons and are not even aware of them, or they just try not to deal with having these feelings, which brings on infidelity if not dealt with. Infidelity is a violation of a couple's assumed or stated contract regarding emotional and sexual exclusivity, such as being unfaithful to spouse or other sexual partner, adultery, disloyalty, falseness, breach of trust, double-dealings, fornication.

Unbelief is what causes a person to fall. Most leaders deal with this because they don't like to believe there's a problem. I've came across a lot of pastors, leaders struggling with spirit sex demons and don't even know why or even if they're attracted to someone, whether it is male or female. They try fighting off these feelings, most of them do because they came to terms with what they're feeling and began to pray. By praying, it will strengthen their spirit. If these things are happening or you feel like this is happening to you, whether you're aware or not that someone is doing this, pray and ask God to wake that person up or to stop a person from lusting and fantasizing about you in their sleep. Sometimes they will stop, if you know who's doing it. If it doesn't stop, it means that it is more than one person having spirit-sex with you. It is not a person's fault but sometimes we get caught up in sin by communicating with this person unaware.

This is how you fight off spirit sex or this sex demons: you must plead the blood of Jesus over your spirit, mind, and body. Plead the blood of Jesus in your bedroom and throughout your house, office, church, and business. Pray to God to send down your angels for protection. A person must speak out loud to their angels because they cannot hear your thoughts. You must ask God to strengthen your spirit because you cannot fight these sex demons off of you being in the flesh, you must be in the spirit. Some people are visited at night in their dreams by human spirits or evil spirits and don't even know. Sometimes these sex spirits come in when you're masturbating while you sleep because these demons are causing you to join your spirit with theirs. Whatever controls their spirit will try and control you. When you have sexual intercourse with a person, the spirit of every person that they had sexual intercourse with gets into your spirit. Whoever you sleep with, all these spirits transfer and become soul ties and spirit ties and will become strongholds in your life. So now that you are aware of these things, you must begin to break these soul ties and spirit ties because they're evil and ungodly ties in your life. If this person is molesting you in your sleep, they might be on assignment from the devil to stop you and pull you away from your purpose (destiny). This person might be friends with you or try to get close to you.

As I wrote earlier, once you give into this sex spirit in your sleep, you have formed a bond unaware. You might think once you meet this person that it is a spiritual relationship because your spirit will be attracted to that person, because this connection happened in your sleep, in the spiritual realm, and it can sometimes come over into the natural realm because this spirit became bonded before you met in the flesh. This spirit is like the flesh, this spirit is like Jezebel's spirit. You might think that person is sent by God because your relationship is a spiritual relationship that's why God says to try the spirit by the spirit to see if it is of God. God's word is his word and God will never go against his written word—the Bible. So please get ready to deal with these spirits if you think they are trying to attack you.

I have written about a lot of spirits in this book, so it can help you identify what spirits are trying to attach itself to a person unaware. A person must be able to identify what spirit is attacking the body, and then begin to break these different types of evil spirits out of your life, give your life to God and repent and or re-dedicate your life back to God.

CHAPTER 12

Deliverance

Deliverance—being delivered.

Deliverance—the action of being rescued or set free.

Deliverance ministry refers to the activity of cleansing a person of demons and evil spirits in order to address problems manifesting in their life, as a result of the presence of said entities and the root cause of their authority to oppress that person.

Deliverance Letter to God

There's a battle going on inside of me, and I can't fight it alone anymore. You said in your word that you will fight my battles because they don't belong to me and if I give them to you, you will fight them for me. Lord, what's happening on the inside of me has become a training ground for the devil. The devil has begun to attack my mind and cause me to have all kinds of thoughts. I know these thoughts cannot be coming from you, but they are trying to take over my mind with thoughts of causing harm to myself and others. These spirits I know are evil. So God, I'm asking you to take control over my mind, my thoughts. Lord, please place in my thoughts love and happiness. Lord, I need you right now to clean my heart, wash all hate, bitterness, anger out of me in the name of Jesus. Lord, don't allow my heart to become cold. Help me, Lord, to bring my flesh under subjection. Take all thoughts of lust, fornication, adultery, and please do not allow that seducing spirit to stay.

Lord, please don't allow pride to come in and try to take over because I know if I have a prideful spirit you can't use me, if I'm greedy, jealous, envious, and hold unforgiveness in my heart. So I'm asking you in your son Jesus's name to take these judgmental, demanding, ruthless, lying, and cheating spirits out of my life. Lord, I do not want to be controlling and manipulating, cunning, because if I am that means I'm allowing the devil to use me and this is a form of witchcraft. Please don't allow me to have any of those spirits inside controlling me and causing me not to walk in love. Lord, I love you. I need you. Please forgive me for all my sins, known and unknown, seen and unseen, because I know you are a loving God who will forgive all of my sins, if I just ask and sin no more. You said that you will forgive us and throw our sins in the sea of forgetfulness, never to return. Lord, in the name of Jesus, I ask that you cover me in your Son's precious blood and continue to watch over my soul because my soul belongs to you. I thank you for healing my body and taking out every spirit that is not like you and that you will protect me from the devil, not allowing him to try and come back to kill, steal, and destroy my destiny. The call that you placed in my life is for your glory and no one else's.

Lord, I thank you for delivering me from the things of this wicked world. I thank you for what you are getting ready to do in my life because now I know that I have been given power to slay dragons and move forward in you. I'm ready, Lord, to do destiny with you. Lord, I know you have called me to help build up your kingdom and for all of these things I thank you.

Love you from deep within, Janet.

Having a Personal Relationship with God

There are prayers of others that can be used but I chose to write a letter of deliverance to God to try to show people that your personal prayers will reach God, your personal prayers should come from your heart, and your personal prayers will go straight to heaven to God. Please seek God. You must have a personal relationship with God in order for God to restore you, no matter what's going on around you, no matter what, stay focused, and get closer to God. Make your walk with God a personal relationship.

Scriptures to Read on Strongholds, Deliverance, and Prayers

2 Corinthians 10:3–4, 2 Samuel 22:2–3, John 10:9–11, James 4:7, Psalms 32:7, 1 Corinthians 15:55–58, Romans 6:14–19, Ephesians 6:10–18, James 5:13–16, Isaiah 43:15–17.

Deliverance Prayers for Spiritual Husband and Wife

Jude 1:7–8, Matthew 22:29–30, Colossians 2:14–15

In order to pray to remove the Spiritual Husband and Wife spirit off your life, you will have to accept that you're in bondage. If you don't accept that you're in bondage, you will stay in bondage. For the Spiritual Husband and Wife deliverance prayer, a person must first fast and pray asking God to deliver you from the Spiritual Husband and Wife in the name of Jesus and repent of all your sins and your forefathers' sins. By doing this, you are breaking generational curses that have been in your family or placed on your family bloodline, asking Jesus to deliver you from the Spiritual Husband and Wife, asking God to break soul ties. These spirits want to destroy your marriage or stop you from marrying. Please pray and ask God to take this spirit off you, so that it will not kill you and take you to hell. Repent for the kingdom of God is at hand. Repent, repent, and repent. God has shown us what the devil is doing so we will not stay in bondage and that we can fight off these evil spirits and get rid of these Spiritual Husband and Wife demons. These demons are watching (soul ties), when a person is sleeping with others causing the transfer of spirits. God will pull you out, God's mercy and grace is on us. We can break free of these evil spirits, we must plead the blood.

The Spiritual Husband and Wife is an illegal relationship that God has shown me. God's word says I am a new creature, a new person in Christ Jesus. It is illegal because angels or spirits are not supposed to marry, so we must shut the doors that the devil has opened up to set a trap for us to be lost. We must come out of captivity. We can come out by pleading the blood of Jesus, because Jesus died for our sins. Pray: Lord Jesus, come into my life. I belong to Jesus, my body, soul, and spirit. You, Husband and Wife spirit, must let me go in the name of Jesus. I no longer belong to you. I'm free in the name of Jesus. I'm free, I'm free, I'm free. I am protected by God in Jesus's name, amen.

REFERENCES

References from the Word of God.
The KJV and the NIV Bible
Ellicott's Commentary of the English Readers
Pastor Alpha Lukau, "Teaching How to Deal with Spirits"
Wikipedia, Define.
Prophet Brain Carn, "Tapping into God's Presents"

CPSIA information can be obtained
at www.ICGtesting.com
Printed in the USA
JSHW032322140422
R11571100001B/R115711PG24842JSX00001B/1